Teach Your Young Child Science
(100 Science Starters)

CW01096026

Teach Your Young Child Science

(**100** Science Starters)

by
Gordon Pemberton

Tynron Press, Scotland

© Gordon Pemberton, 1989

First published in 1989 by
Tynron Press
Stenhouse
Thornhill
Dumfriesshire

ISBN 1-871948-36-3
All rights reserved

Cover and illustrations by Paul O'Shea
Typeset by A-Z Graphic
Printed by Sing Chew Press Pte Ltd, Singapore

Note For Parents

Until recent years it was thought that children were too young to study science until they reached the secondary school, with its well-equipped laboratories and its specialist teachers. But now it is known that young children can appreciate many of the scientific phenomena they see around them, in their homes and their environment. They do not need laboratories or even teachers to be able to observe and understand many of the effects of basic scientific principles.

For instance, evaporation takes place on a washing line; condensation can be seen when you get a cold bottle of Coke from the fridge; floatation can easily be demonstrated with a jar and a bucket of water; capillary attraction can be shown using a saucer of water and a core of toilet roll!

In this three-part booklet are **100** simple scientific activities and experiments which can all be done easily at home or in the family environment.

Part 1 invites the child to learn about the world around him through the close examination and manipulation of a range of everyday materials. The suggested activities are by no means exhaustive, but should help stimulate children to follow other avenues of exploration either on their own initiative, or as prompted by their parents.

Part 2 introduces the child to the basic principles of physical science — weight, density, volume, pressure, friction, etc. — through a series of simple experiments.

Part 3 continues with a range of experiments which also cover earth and biological sciences. Here many of the experiments involve recording developments over longer periods of time, or under particular weather conditions.

In each section, the 'scientific apparatus' required consists of nothing more complicated than bottles, jars, bowls, buckets, boxes, tins, sticks, forks, spoons, nails, old coins and other items — all of which are to be found at home, or obtained easily and cheaply.

All that is really required is a parent who can spare a few minutes each day for the advancement of a young child in basic education.

Part 1

Looking at Materials
From the World Around Us

1 Paper: tissues, toilet paper, paper bags, duplicating paper, blotting paper, serviettes, manila envelopes, typing paper, copy paper, writing paper, cartridge paper, sugar paper, kitchen paper, greaseproof paper, newspaper, wrapping paper, waxed paper, etc..

Fold it — does it stay in folds?

Tear it — does it tear easily? Look at the tear with your magnifying glass.

Pull it — does it stay stiff, does it stretch or does it break?

Write on it — is it good or bad for writing on?

Roll it into a tube — is it strong?

Wet it — what happens?

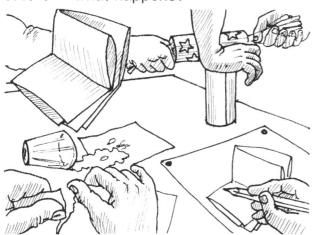

2 Threads & String: cotton, linen, nylon, rayon, coarse wool, fine wool, thin string, thick string, coarse string, picture cord, nylon cord, thin rope, thick rope.

Feel it — smooth or rough, thick or thin?

Pull it (use gloves) — weak, strong or very strong?

Look at it through the magnifying glass. What is it made of?

Tie a knot in it. Is this easy or difficult — why?

3 **Woven or Knitted Materials:** pieces of cloth taken from old clothes and household materials. Choose a range of fabrics from superfine to very coarse and, if possible, a variety of patterns and types of weave from simple to complicated. (Attractive colours add incentive to the work to be done.)

Look at the material through a magnifying glass. What is it like? Look again. Can you see each thread? Look at the edge.
Can you see the ways the threads go?

Feel it — is it coarse or fine? Could you wear it on your skin?
Pull it gently — is it strong or weak?

4 **Springy Materials:** natural sponge, plastic sponge, plastic foam, soft rubber ball, rubber rings (quoits), rubber bands, etc..

Look — any patterns?
Feel it — hard or soft, stiff or flexible?
Pull or bend it — does it stretch; does it lose shape; does it come back to shape?
Drop it — does it bounce?

3

5 **Sounds:** containers of all kinds — bottles, tins, jars, plastic containers, pieces of wood, metal and synthetics. A drumstick. (A chopstick, knitting needle or even a pencil will do equally well.)

Bang each one — what sounds are made? Which ones make dull sounds and which ones ringing sounds?

Half fill each with sand. Is the sound made the same?

Fill to the top with sand. Is the sound the same?

6 **Rocks:** small samples of rocks — sandstone, limestone, pumice, slate, marble, quartz, granite, conglomerate, etc., each about the size of a hen's egg.

Look — any patterns? Look at all of them. What differences can you see?

Hold it — heavy or light?
Feel it — hard or crumbly, rough or smooth?
Put water on it — what happens?

7 Wooden Materials: hardwood, soft-wood, bark, ruler, piece of branch, cross-section of a trunk, balsa, cork, matches (used), spills, etc..

Feel it — rough or smooth, hard or soft, stiff or flexible?
Look — can you see lines or patterns?

Try to bend it — strong or weak?
Smell — do they all smell the same?

8 Metals: small pieces (flat if possible) of iron, steel, copper, brass, bronze, aluminium, coins, eating utensils, small containers, ornaments, steel wool, magnet.

Look — shiny or dull?
Rub with steel wool — shiny or dull underneath?

Hold it — heavy or light?
Feel it — rough or smooth, stiff or flexible?
Does it stick to the magnet or not?

9 **Glass:** all glass articles should be fairly solid to lessen the risk of fracture — small thick sheet (mirror size), prisms, stoppers, lens, small thick jar, round plain bottle, glass marble, rod.

Look — what shape?
Feel it — rough or smooth, stiff or flexible?
Look through it at a book page — what do you see? Now look through it at a leaf, carpet, curtain — what do you see?

10 **Looking Closely:** a good magnifying glass and a collection of stones, wood, fabric, sponge, loofah, and other pieces of interesting materials.

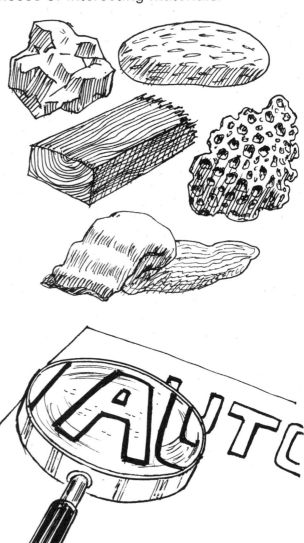

Use the glass to observe all the objects closely to see what they are made of and how they are made. Also look at the pictures and print in books, newspapers and comics, and ordinary writing with pencil and pen.

11 **Opaque Materials:** wood, metals, thick cloth, cardboard, thick paper, leather, etc.. Different objects and shapes, some containers and some not. (This activity is best done just before or just after No. 12.)

12 **Transparent Synthetics:** perspex, acetate, polythene in varying grades of thickness. Different shapes and objects made from these materials. Some should be containers and some not; some coloured and some plain.

Feel it — rough or smooth, hard or soft, stiff or flexible?
Put it on a book — can you see through it?
Hold it up to the light — can you see through it?
Half fill it with water — can you see the level of the water?

Feel it — rough or smooth, hard or soft, stiff or flexible?
Put it on a book — can you see through it?
Half fill it with water — can you see the level of the water?

13 **Colours:** a selection of pieces of transparent plastic, in these colours — red, blue, green, yellow, pink, orange, purple, brown.

Look through it at a book — easy or hard to see the print?

Look through it at the light — does it show light or dark?

Put any two together and look at the light. What new colour do you see? Try more of these; what new clours do you see?

Try any three together — what do you see?

14 **Pipes:** rubber tubing, rubber hose, plastic hose, plastic drain-pipe, copper pipe, cardboard roll, drinking straws, etc..

Feel it — rough or smooth, hard or soft, stiff or flexible?

Look through it — can you see anything?

Blow through it — what do you feel at the other end?

Can you pour water through it?

15 **A Feeling Game:** a collection of everyday objects — bottle, spoon, sponge, pencil, book, etc., and a blindfold.

Put on the blindfold.
Feel each object in turn and say what you think it is. How many did you get right?

16 **Looking At Living Things:** a good magnifying glass and a collection of twigs, leaves, flowers, etc..
Use the glass to observe the different parts of the leaves, twigs and flowers. Also use the glass to observe hands, knees, arms, legs and (with great care) ears, nose and eyes.

17 **Another Feeling Game:** four different sized cubes (e.g. building blocks, tissue boxes, etc.). Six different sized tins.

Put on a blindfold.
Put the four cubes in order from smallest to largest. Do the same with the six tins. Did you get them right each time?

18 **Reflecting Surfaces:** small mirror, metal cylinder, large ball bearing, large shiny spoon, various items in copper and brass, all shiny and some with irregular surfaces if possible.

Look at your reflection in each in turn —what do you see?
Separate those items which make you look peculiar. Which ones are best for reflecting properly?

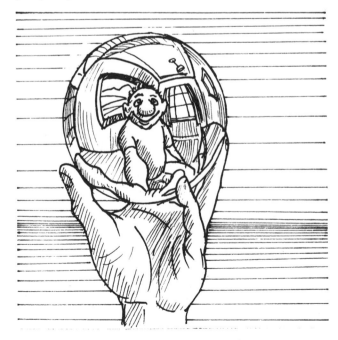

19 **More Sounds:** containers of tin and other metals, plastic, acetate, etc..
A drumstick. (A chopstick, knitting needle or even a pencil will do equally well.)
Hit each container with a stick — what sound is made?

Put a little water in — does it sound the same? Try each one like this.
Fill it half-full with water — how does the sound alter? Now fill it to the top with water — how does it sound? Try each one like this.

Pick out those which make the best sounds. Can you put them in order from low sounds to high sounds?

20 **Weighing For Density:** jars (all the same size) of nuts, peas, beans, rice, sand, water.

Fill each jar with something different and then compare the weight of each using kitchen scales. (If you have, or can improvise, a set of pan-scales, try weighing each jar against crude weights such as marbles or same-sized pebbles.)

Put them in order of weight from lightest to heaviest.

Part 2

Some Simple Experiments
Using Everyday Items

21 You need a jar, a spoon and some salt.

Half-fill the jar with water. Put your finger in and taste the water. Now add one spoonful of salt to the water. Stir the water until it is clear again. Can you see the salt now?

Put your finger in again and taste the water. Where has the salt gone?

22 You need one small bottle.

Fill the bottle with water at the washbasin. Turn the bottle over very slowly. Let the water out very slowly.

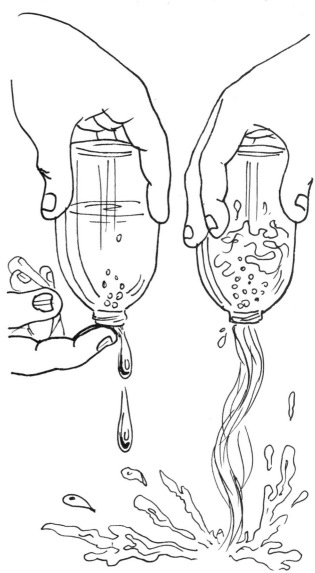

Fill the bottle again. Turn it upside down quickly and let the water pour out as fast as it can.

Was the first time different from the second time? Can you think why?

23 You need a piece of wood, a piece of sandpaper, a small tin box, a nail.

Rub the wood very hard with the sandpaper. Feel them both.
What do you feel?

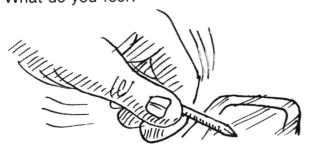

Rub the tin box hard with the end of the nail. Feel them both.
What do you feel?

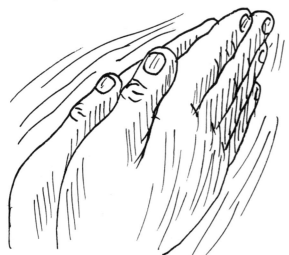

Rub your hands together very hard. What do you feel?

24 You need a jar, some metal washers (rings) and a drying cloth.
Fill the jar to the top with water.
Guess how many rings you can put in before the water spills over.

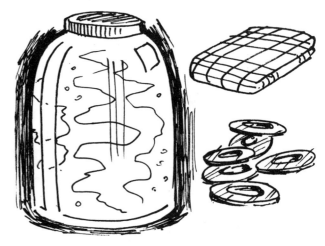

Put the first ring in very carefully. Put more rings in. How many rings did you get in before it spilled?

Did you guess right?

14

25 You need a jar, a piece of sticky paper, some marbles or pebbles.
Half-fill the jar with water. Stick the paper on the jar to show the level of the water. Carefully put a marble into the jar.
Look at the water level.
Put marbles into the jar carefully, one at a time. Watch the level of the water. What happens to it? Can you think why this happens?

26 You need three small bottles with screw tops, and a bucket of water.
Fill the first bottle with water. Screw on the top. Half-fill the second bottle with water. Screw on the top. Put nothing in the third bottle. Screw on the top.

Put the full bottle into the water in the bucket. What happens? Why?
Put the half-full bottle into the water. What happens? Why?
Put the empty bottle into the water. What happens? Why?

15

27 You need a jar, some marbles (or pebbles) and a bucket of water.
Put six marbles into the jar. Lower the jar into the water in the bucket.

Carefully put another marble into the floating jar. Keep putting more marbles into the jar. What happens in the end? Why?

28 You need a bottle and a bucket of water.
Put the empty bottle into the water in the bucket. Let the bottle fill with water and sink.

Turn the bottle upside down under the water. Bring the bottle (still upside down) near to the top of the water. Bring it out of the water except for the very last bit at the neck. Does the water in the bottle spill out?

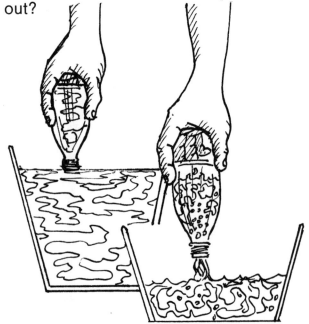

Now lift the whole of the bottle out of the water. Does the water spill out of the bottle now? Why do you think these things happen?

29 You need a jar of water, some small crystals* and a wooden rod.

Put one tiny crystal into the water. What happens?

Use your rod to stir the water. Keep stirring it. What happens to the crystal? What happens to the water?

* The crystals can be potassium permanganate, or some other type of crystals — such as jelly or bath crystals — which will dissolve quickly and colour the water.

30 You need a bowl of water and a piece of transparent, plastic tubing about 50 cm long.

Put the tube in the bowl. Fill it with water. Take hold of each end and lift the tube out of the water. Hold it up so that it makes a letter 'U'. Look at the two water levels at each end of the tube. Are they level with each other?

Move one hand slowly upwards. What happens to the water levels? Move the other hand slowly upwards. What happens to the water levels?

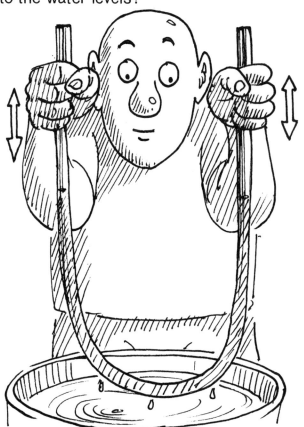

Move one hand slowly downwards. Do the levels stay the same? Move the other hand downwards. Do the levels stay the same? Why do you think this happens?

31 You need an empty bowl, a jug of water, a bottle and a plastic funnel. Stand the empty bottle in the empty bowl. Fill the jug with water then pour the contents straight into the bottle. Was this easy or difficult?

Empty the bottle and stand it again in the empty bowl. Put the funnel into the neck of the bottle. Now fill the bottle again, using the jug and the funnel. Was this easier or more difficult? Why?

32 You need a suction cup (as on a toy arrow or towel holder) and a little water.

Try to stick the dry suction cup to your table top. Try sticking it to the wall and other flat places.

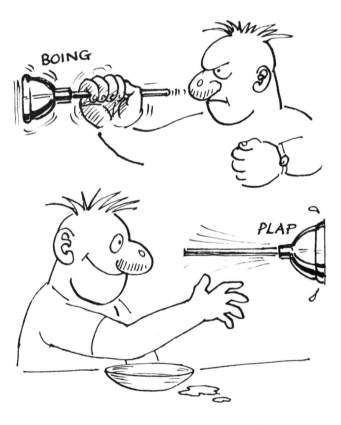

Now wet the suction cup all over at the bottom. Try sticking it to all the places again. Is it better or worse? Why?

33 You need a balloon.

Blow up the balloon. Hold the opening near your cheek. Keep hold of the balloon, but let the air out slowly. What happens? What can you feel?

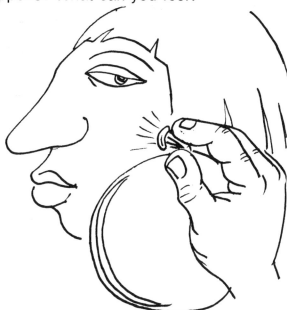

Blow the balloon up again. Hold it as high as you can and then let go of it. What happens? Why do you think this happens?

34 You need a long, thin piece of paper (20cm × 2cm), a paper fastener or clip.

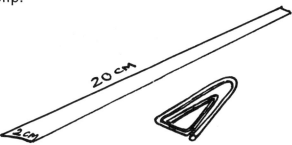

Fold the paper in half across the middle. Put the paper fastener near the fold in the paper. Pull the pieces slightly apart to make a 'V' shape.

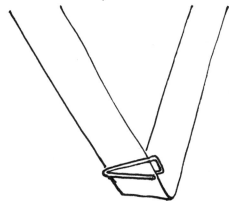

Stand up on a chair. Hold up what you have made and let go of it. What happens? What is it like?

35 You need a drinking straw, a jar of water and a partner to help.

Ask your partner to blow bubbles into the jar of water using the straw. Watch the bubbles closely.
Ask him to blow bubbles as slowly as he can. Watch the bubbles closely.

Ask him to blow very small puffs. Watch these bubbles closely. What is in the bubbles? Why do they come to the top?

36 You need a short drinking glass, a drinking straw and a bowl of water.

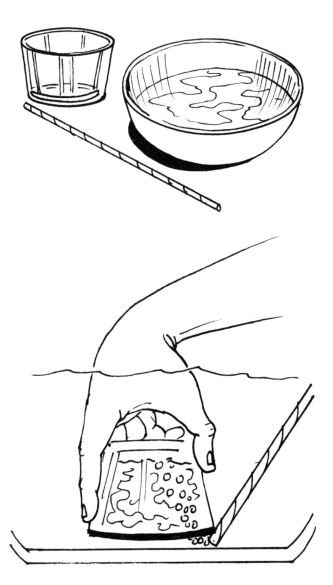

Put the glass into the bowl of water and let it sink. Turn it upside down under the water. Hold it just above the bottom of the bowl. With your straw, blow bubbles under it. What happens? Why do you think this happens?

20

37 You need a mirror, a large sheet of plain paper, a pencil and a book.

Write your name on the sheet of paper in big letters. Turn your back to the paper. Hold up the mirror and look at your name in it. What has the mirror done to your name? Why?

Put your mirror upright on a page of the book. Look at the words in the mirror. What does the mirror do to the letters? Does it do this to other things? Try it and see.

38 You need a mug, a coin, a jug of water and a partner.

Put the mug on a table with the coin in the bottom of it. Stand where you can just see the coin in the mug. Step back a little until the coin disappears from your sight.

Now ask your partner to pour water into the mug. Keep watching the mug. What happens? Can you think why this happens? (Watch your partner's legs next time he goes down the swimming pool steps!)

39 You need a long nail, a jar and a jug of water.

Stand the nail in the jar. Pour water into the jar. Watch the nail as you pour the water. What seems to happen to it?
Move the nail about. What do you see?

40 You need a large shiny spoon.

Stand with your back to a window.
Look at your face in the back of the spoon.
What do you see?

Look at your face in the front of the spoon. What do you see?
Look at your face in other curved, shiny things. How does it look?

41 You need a black bowl (or dark-coloured container) and a jug of water.

Put the container near a window. Half-fill it with water. Wait until the water is still. Look at your face in the water.

Use your finger to make the water move a little. What happens to your face in the water?

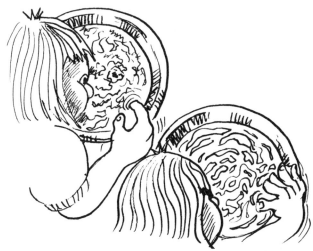

Stir the water till it goes round. What happens to your face now?

42 You need a large bottle.
Blow gently across the top of the bottle. You should hear a deep sound.

Now put a little water into the bottle and blow across the top again. What has happened to the sound?
Put some more water into the bottle and blow across the top. What has happened to the sound?

Keep putting more water into the bottle and blowing across the top each time. What happens each time? Can you think why?

43 You need some forks of different sizes.

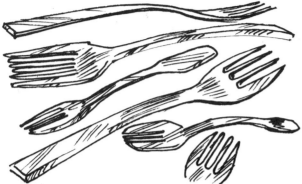

Take the biggest fork and bang the prongs on your table. Quickly stand the fork on its end on the table. Listen to the sound it makes.

Do this with the next biggest fork. Is the sound higher or lower? Do it with all the other forks, in order of size. What do you notice about the sounds the forks make?

44 You need four tins of different sizes and a pencil.

Put the tins in order, the biggest first. Tap the biggest with your pencil. Listen to the sound. Tap the next tin with your pencil. Is the sound lower or higher?
Tap the other tins and listen to each in turn. What do you notice about the sounds of the four tins?

45 You need a bicycle pump.

Pull the pump right out. Put your mouth near the air hole and blow across it so that you make a sound. While you are blowing, move the handle upwards. What happens to the sound? Can you find out why this happens?

46 You need a magnet, a jar, a small box and some paper clips.

Take the magnet round the room. Touch many things with it. What kinds of things does it stick to?

Put the magnet into the small box. Bring the box near to the paper clips. What happens to the clips?

Put the magnet into the jar. Bring the jar near the paper clips.
What happens to the clips?

47 You need a bowl of water, a magnet and some paper clips.

48 You need a Toblerone packet, a ruler, some coins, some modelling clay or Plasticine.

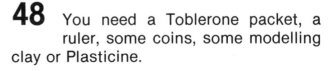

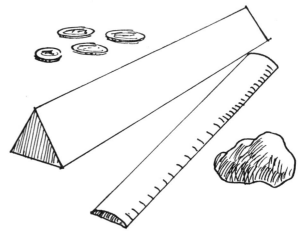

Drop the clips into the bowl of water. Put the magnet into the water. Will it pull the clips out?
Try other things in the water. Will the magnet pull them out?

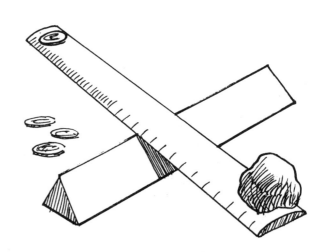

Put the ruler on the Toblerone packet. Make it like a see-saw. Put a coin at one end of the ruler. Put enough clay on the other end to balance it.
Now put the coin nearer the middle. Does it need more or less clay to balance it? Try this with different sized coins, some at the end of the ruler, some near the middle.

49 You need six cubes of different sizes, a blindfold and a partner.

Put on the blindfold. Your friend will give you all the cubes, mixed up. Without looking, find the biggest. Put the cubes in order of size, biggest to smallest.

Let your partner mix the cubes up again and give them to you. This time, find the smallest first and put them in order, smallest to biggest.

50 You need four cups, a jug of water, a small towel, a blindfold and a partner.
Put on the blindfold so that you cannot see and ask your partner to pour a different amount of water into each cup.

With the help of your partner, put your finger into each cup.
Which has the most water? Put the cups in order, from most water to least water.

Let your partner mix up the cups again. This time, put your finger in each cup and find the one with least water. Put the cups in order from least water to most water.

Part 3

BEANS

More Experiments and Scientific Activities

Water

51 Put separate drops of water onto a plate. Leave the plate in the window. The drops disappear. Where do they go? Compare with puddles after rain. Do the same with drops of coloured water. The water evaporates, but leaves the colour behind.

52 Split the end of a used matchstick and carefully make it into a narrow 'V'.
Put a drop of washing-up liquid into the 'V' and place the match in a bowl of water.
The match will move forward. The washing-up liquid pushes the water back, and so the match moves forward

53 Stick pieces of tape at the same level on each of two small jars. Fill each jar with water to the level marked. Put a foil cover on one of the jars, and put them both in a warm place. What happens in a few hours?

54 Pour a small bucket of water onto concrete or paving stones on a hot, sunny day.

In the open one, some of the water has turned into vapour (evaporated) and escaped into the air. In the other, the foil cover has prevented evaporation and so no water has escaped.

After a few moments, the process of evaporation can be seen around the edges of the wet patch.

55 Pour some water into a shallow saucer. Add a few drops of colouring (ink). Stand a toilet-roll core upright in the water. Leave it for a while and watch what happens. What does happen?

56 Split the stem of a large white flower. Place two containers, one filled with blue coloured water and the other filled with red coloured water, side by side. Put one part of the split stem into each container.

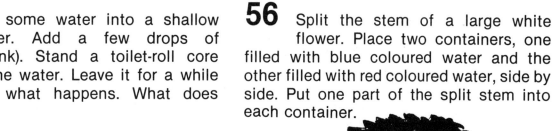

After some hours the flower will show both red and blue colouring.

57 In a saucer mix one teaspoonful of salt with a little water, until the salt has dissolved. Leave this in a window for a few hours. What happens?

Now try this using sugar instead of salt. Does the same happen?

58 Put a bottle of water (or Coke etc.) in the fridge for an hour or two. Take it out and put it on the table. What happens?

Feel it with your finger. Where do you think the water came from?

59 Put a small mirror into the fridge and leave it there for an hour or two. Take it out and put it on the table. What happens? Run your finger across it. Where do you think the water came from this time?

60 Crumple a piece of paper and wedge it into the bottom of a dry glass. Press the glass, upside down, into a bowl of water.

The paper will not get wet because of the air trapped in the glass.

61 Get some jars and half-fill them with water. Into the jars, put pieces of plastic sponge, natural sponge, thin card, thick card, wood, fibre board, etc..

After a few hours look at them and see what has happened.

62 Carefully lower a fresh egg into a glass of fresh water and it will sink to the bottom.

Take the egg out and stir three tablespoonfuls of salt into the water until it disappears.

Replace the egg and it will float half-way down the glass, showing that salt water is more buoyant than fresh water.

63 Fill a small, narrow-necked bottle with water right to the top. Put on a loose-fitting foil cap. Put the bottle in the freezer compartment of the fridge.

Next day you will find a column of ice coming out of the neck, showing that frozen water expands and takes up more space.

64 Put an ice cube in a glass and fill the glass to the very top with water. The ice will float.

When the ice melts, will the water overflow? No, because when the ice becomes water again, it needs less space.

65 Sprinkle some black pepper onto a saucer of water. With a wet bar of soap, touch the water near the edge. The floating pepper will rush away from the bar of soap, showing the destruction of the surface 'skin' of the water by the soap.

66 Soak two small pieces of cloth in water. Put one in an open jar and the other in a tightly-closed jar. Put both jars in a warm place.

1 hour later

After an hour look at the two jars. What **has** happened? Can you tell why?

Out of Doors

67 During a wet spell, stick a piece of paper, with graduations in centimetres, on a glass jar. Put the jar outside.

Measure the rainfall at the end of each day, then empty the jar, ready for the next day's rain.

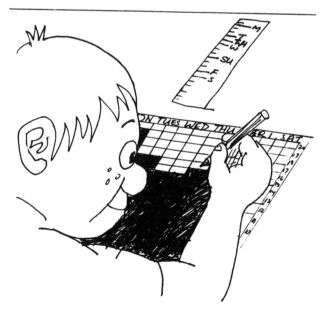

Record the week's rainfall in a simple block graph on squared paper.

68 Fasten a long, thick stick — like a broom or mop handle — upright to a small chair on a hard surface on a very sunny day. Draw a chalk line down its shadow.

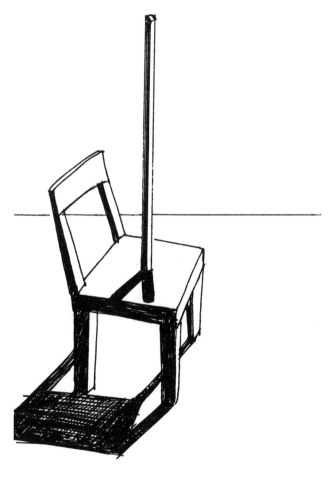

Come back an hour later. What has happened to the shadow? Draw another line down the new shadow. Compare the two lines for direction and length.

69 Do the same with a friend. Draw a circle for him to stand in with his back to the sun. Draw a chalk line round his shadow.

Come back an hour later and draw his new shadow. Compare the two shadows for direction and length.

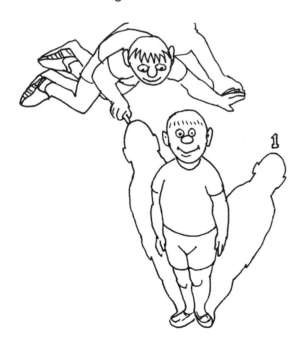

70 Go to a park or group of trees. Observe the leaves and the buds.

Observe the trunks and the bark. Note any differences in colour, shape, pattern or texture.

Make sketches to show the differences.

71 Go to a pond or lake. Make sure you have an adult with you in case you slip into the water.

Choose an interesting part and mark off ten paces. Observe all the water plants that can be seen. Can any water life be seen?

72 On a visit to the beach, choose an interesting part (perhaps one which has rock pools). Mark off ten paces.

What plant and bird life can be seen? Can you see any water life? Make notes of the things you see and bring back any interesting seaweed, stones, shells or small pieces of rock to examine at home.

73 Make a sun-clock. Take a piece of wood about 30cm square. Bore a hole near the edge, half-way along one side. Stand a straight stick (dowel) about 30cm long in the hole. Point the stick-side of your 'clock' towards the sun in the morning and mark the stick-shadow on the hour, each hour of the day.

74 You can also make a water-clock. Make a tiny hole in the bottom of a tall, plastic bottle. Stick a strip of paper down the side of the bottle. Fill the bottle with water but leave the top open. Hang up the bottle where the drips will not matter and make a water-level mark on the paper strip every hour.

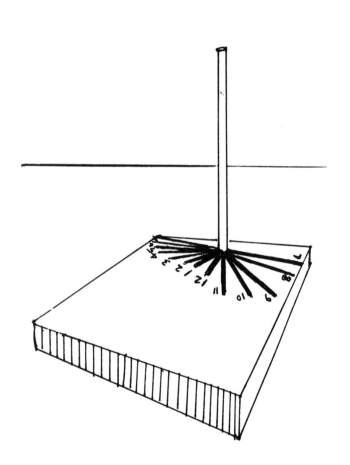

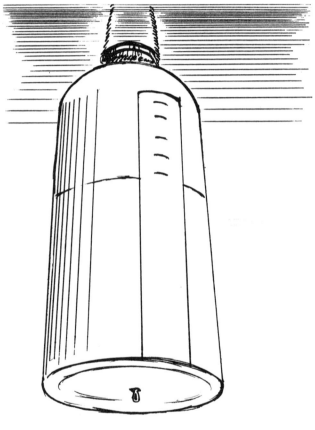

Next day, you will be able to tell the time by your sun-clock, without looking at an ordinary clock. (This experiment will show better results if done towards the middle or end of the year.)

Next day, after filling the bottle again, you will be able to tell the time without looking at an ordinary clock.

75 Make four small heaps of (a) soil (b) sand (c) clay (d) gravel, on four old trays or boards. Put them outside when heavy rain is expected.

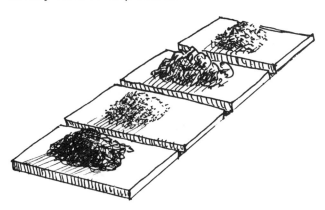

What does the rain do to them? What does heavy rain do to piles of earth, banks, and earth on sloping ground?

Plants and Seeds

76 Put a small plant in the ground or in a plant pot. Take a piece of plastic drain-pipe about 25cm long. Stand this over the plant and leave it open at the top. Make sure that the earth round the plant is kept damp.

What happens in a few days? Why?

77 Germinate peas and beans in jam jars lined with damp blotting paper. See that they do not become too dry. Grow similar peas and beans in small fibre pots or used yoghurt cartons.

78 Put the seeds of annuals — such as marigolds, petunias, celosia (chee kwan hwa) — in soil-filled fibre pots. The seeds can be bought at any supermarket.

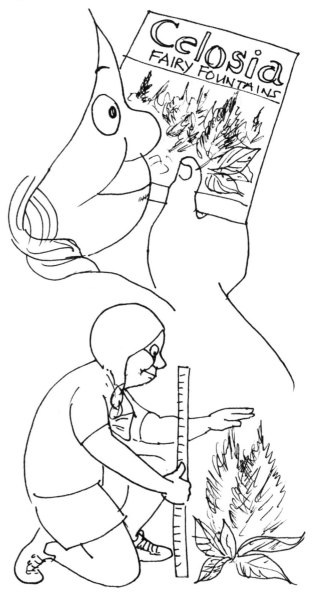

Plant them in the ground when they are strong enough.

Put the plants into the ground when they are strong enough and keep a record of how much they grow upwards each day.

79 In soil-filled fibre pots, grow whole grains such as wheat, barley, maize, etc.. The grain can be bought at health-food shops.

Put them in the ground when they are strong enough.

80 Grow climbing beans or plants — long beans, morning glory, sweet pea, money plants — in fibre pots filled with soil. The plants can be trained to grow up the side of the house or up tall sticks.

81 Grow orange pips, plum stones, avocado stones and any other unusual seeds in potting mixture. Such seeds take a long time to germinate, so patience is required. With care, the plants that grow from such 'stones' can last for many years.

82 Quick-germinating seeds such as water-cress are simple to grow. Sprinkle the seeds on damp tissue paper or cotton wool. (Do not make the paper etc. too wet.)

83 Put two similar plants in small pots. Water them both well then put one in the window and the other in a dark cupboard for a few days. What happens? (The plants can be weeds from the garden or locality, as long as they are similar in type and size.)

84 Get two similar plants; they can be weeds as in experiment 83. Water them both then put one in a polythene bag and fasten it to make it airtight.

Put both plants in the window for a few days. What happens?

45

85 To show how new plants can be grown from existing plants, put cuttings of plants and twigs in suitable compost in fibre or yoghurt pots. Episcea, geraniums, bougainvillea and spider plants are good for this.

86 Slice the top off a carrot or parsnip. Put it in a saucer of water and keep it fairly wet.

When growth is strong, transfer the plants to the ground.

In a few days, small buds will appear and these will eventually grow into a 'fern'.

87 Fill a small jar with water. Rest an onion on the rim of the jar so that the bottom of the onion just touches the surface of the water.

88 Fill several tall jars with water; rain water would be best. Put budded twigs of different trees into the jars. If the buds come into leaf and grow strong root systems, they can be put into pots of soil.

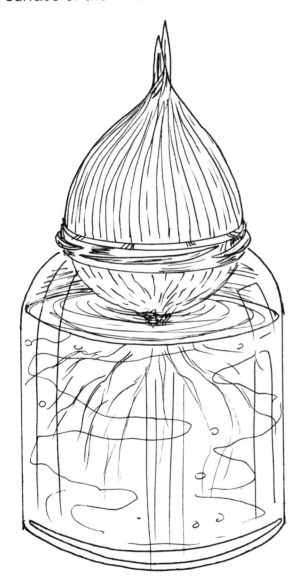

Keep the level of the water topped up and the onion will grow. Plant it in a pot when the root system is strong enough.

89 A large, sealed jar or fish tank can demonstrate a completely enclosed cycle of plant living.

Cover the base with soil and bed out a selection of plants. Water the plants and then seal the jar. (No further water, or air, is needed.)

Temperature

90 Fill two small screw-top jars with hot water. Screw on the caps and put one jar into a cardboard box filled with sawdust or crumpled paper.

A little advice on the best plants to use and the upkeep of the enclosed garden from your local nursery or plant dealer, will ensure amazing results.

After half an hour, feel the side of each jar. What do you find? The jar which was in the box (insulated) should be hotter.

91 Get two small, identical plastic containers. Put dry soil into one, and water into the other. Place a thermometer in each bowl and sit the bowls in the sun. Read the thermometers to find out which becomes hotter more quickly.

Now, put the containers in a cool place and see which becomes cooler quicker.

92 Get a small bottle and fit an unfilled balloon over its neck. Place the upright bottle into a bowl of hot water. What happens? (The balloon inflates slightly, showing that warm air takes up more space.)

Empty the hot water from the bowl and replace it with cold water. Put the bottle into this cold water. What happens to the balloon? (It deflates because the air in the bottle has become cooler and so takes up less space.)

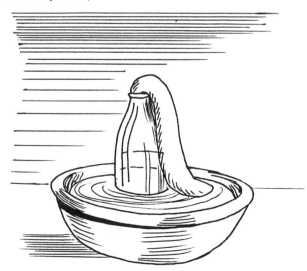

49

93 Into a cup of hot water, put a metal spoon.

After a short time, feel the handle. It has become hot.

Now put a plastic spoon into the hot water. Does it become as hot as the metal spoon? (No, because it is not as good a conductor of heat as metal.)

How Things Change

94 Put a piece of cooking fat, such as butter, margarine or ghee, on a saucer and leave it in the warmest place you can find. What happens to it?

Now put it in the fridge for a few hours. What happens?

95 Put a large iron nail into a jar half-full of water. Put another nail into an empty jar. Leave them side-by-side.

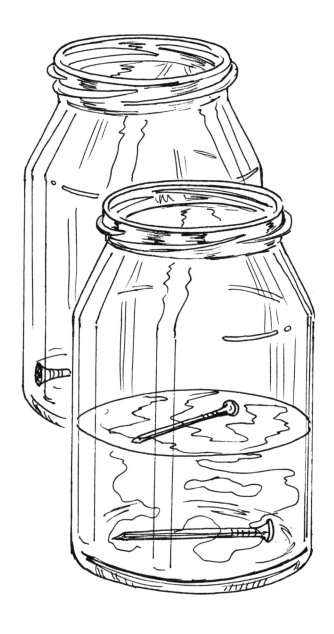

After a few days, examine both nails. Does the same thing happen to each nail?

96 Put small pieces of cheese, vegetables, fruit and bread on a saucer and leave them for a few days where they cannot be eaten by ants, birds, etc..

BURP!

After a few days, use a magnifying glass to examine what has happened to them.

97 Mix a small amount of yeast with a teaspoonful of sugar in a bowl. Stir in about half a cupful of lukewarm water and two or three cupfuls of flour. Mix everything well to form a dough. Put a cloth over the basin and leave it to rise in a warm place for about an hour.

Yeast is a tiny plant and, in favourable conditions of warmth, water and food, it grows rapidly, creating carbon dioxide, which forms little bubbles in the dough. You can make it into bread by kneading the risen mixture and letting it rise again before baking it.

98 Get two, old one-cent coins which have a similar colour and appearance. Put one into a jar and cover it with vinegar. Put the other into another jar and cover it with plain water. Sit the jars side-by-side and leave them for about a week.

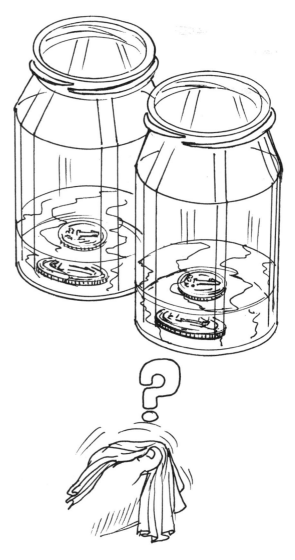

Take each coin out and rub it hard with a piece of cloth. What has happened? Do they both look the same?

99 Fill a plant pot with very dry soil. Put in as much as you can and keep pressing it down as you fill it.

100 Fold two sheets of A4 paper into eight and cut out the pieces. Clip the sixteen small pieces together.

On the first piece, draw a small circle. On the next, a bigger circle, and so on, each circle slightly bigger, with the circle on the last piece the biggest.

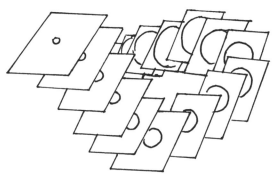

Now flick the pages over rapidly and you will see your little circle 'grow' into a big circle. This is how cartoons are made.

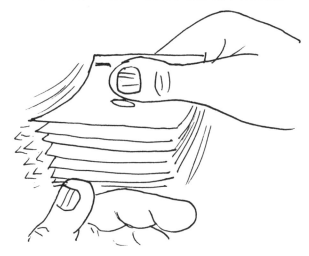

Stand the pot in a saucer containing a little water. Keep the small amount of water in the saucer topped up. Keep feeling the top of the soil in the pot, every half-hour. What happens in the end?